Pop Music

Michael Burnett

Oxford University Press
Music Department,
Walton Street, Oxford OX2 6DP

Contents

1 Where pop came from

Rock 'n' roll *4*
The beginnings of rock 'n' roll *5*
The recipe of rock 'n' roll *6*

From rock 'n' roll to the Beatles *7*
Rhythm 'n' blues *8*
Skiffle *9*
Questions and projects *6, 9, 10*

2 The Beatles, the Stones and Dylan

The Beatles *12*
Early influences *12*
'The world's top group' *13*
Change of style *13*
The end *14*

The Rolling Stones *16*
Britain as a centre of pop music *17*
Questions and projects *15, 17*

Bob Dylan *18*
Protest *18*
Dylan and the Beatles *20*

Folk rock *21*
The West Coast sound *22*
Questions and projects *20, 22*

Pop in 1967 *23*
The Monterey Festival *23*
Super albums *24*

After 1967 *25*
Questions and projects *24, 25*

3 The influences on pop

Pop and jazz *27*
Riffs *27*

Pop and folk music *28*

Pop and classical music *29*
Classical instruments *29*

Pop and electronic music *30*
Feedback *30*
Questions and projects *27, 28, 29, 31*

4 Pop styles today: from folk to punk rock

Hard rock *33*
Rhythm 'n' blues *33*
Rock 'n' roll *33*
Punk rock *34*
Commercial pop *34*
Soul *35*
Reggae *36*
Folk *36*

The solo singer *37*
Progressive *37*
Experimental *38*
Questions and projects *38*

5 The electric band and the recording business

Amplification *40*
Problems of loudness *40*
System of amplification *41*

The instruments of pop *41*
Electric instruments *41*
Acoustic instruments *42*

The recording studio *43*
Studio acoustics *43*
Mixing *43*
How much does it cost? *45*
How a record is made *45*

The Top Thirty *46*
The hit single *46*
How many will it sell? *47*
Questions and projects *41, 42, 45, 47*

Some important names and events *48*

Discography *Inside back cover*

1 Where pop came from

Rock 'n' roll

Over 20 years ago a new sort of music became popular amongst young people in America and Europe. This new music was simple in style, lively and loud. It soon became known as **rock 'n' roll**.

The first star of rock 'n' roll was **Bill Haley**, who, with his band the Comets, recorded *Shake, rattle and roll* in 1954, and, soon after, *Rock around the clock,* which was one of the greatest successes ever.

Bill Haley and the Comets in *Rock around the Clock*

Elvis Presley

But even this was outdone by the successes of a younger star, **Elvis Presley.** His records, such as *Jailhouse rock* and *Blue suede shoes*, had made him even more popular than Bill Haley by 1956, and his moody looks and lively stage performances made him an idol for the teenagers of the 50s.

But what is rock 'n' roll and where did it come from?

The beginnings of rock 'n' roll

In 1954 rock 'n' roll seemed to be completely new, but we can see now that it really came from a mixture of two other sorts of American music: **rhythm 'n' blues** and **country 'n' western**.

The first of these, *rhythm 'n' blues*, was performed by black musicians, such as Howlin' Wolf and Muddy Waters, in the cities of America. Early rock 'n' roll musicians copied its loudness and liveliness, and took from it loud instruments such as electric guitar and saxophone. They also took the chords and framework of the blues and made this the basis of rock 'n' roll (see the diagram of *See you later, alligator* on page 6).

Country 'n' western music—the second part of the rock 'n' roll mixture—was performed by white musicians, usually in the West and middle West of America. It was quieter and less lively than rhythm 'n' blues. Often it took the form of cowboy songs accompanied by acoustic guitar, banjo and string bass. The nose-pinching voices of many rock 'n' roll stars came from country 'n' western music, together with the simple tunes and easily remembered choruses popular with teenagers in 1954–56.

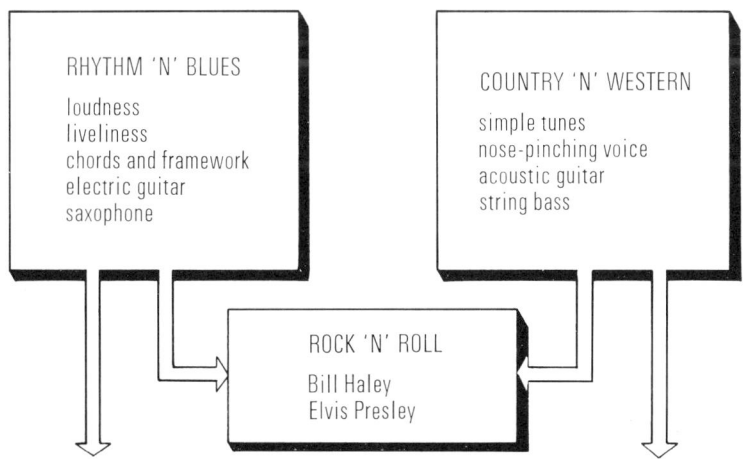

Little Richard in action

Bill Haley and Elvis Presley were, of course, not the only stars of rock 'n' roll. Some of the most successful were performers who had started as rhythm 'n' blues singers, such as **Chuck Berry** and **Little Richard**. Few people could put together the ingredients of rock 'n' roll in a more exciting way than Little Richard, whose record *Tutti Frutti* sold over a million copies in 1955. Here's a description of him on stage:

> He played piano and he'd stand knock-kneed at the keyboard, hammering away with two hands as if he wanted to bust the thing apart . . . He'd scream and scream and scream. He had a freak voice . . . On every phrase he'd embroider with squeals, rasps, siren whoops . . .

N. COHN *Pop from the beginning* Weidenfeld and Nicolson

The recipe of rock 'n' roll

Take three simple **chords** and spread them out over twelve bars (or boxes) by repeating each one a number of times. Each bar has four **beats** in it. The final ingredient, the most tasty, is the **tune** which goes on top of the chords.

A rock 'n' roll record will consist of several repeats of the twelve bar set of chords and tune. At least once the tune will be left out and, instead, there will be an instrumental solo.

One of the most common arrangements of the three chords is the one Bill Haley uses in *See you later, alligator*, so we'll take that as an example.

count	①2 3 4	②2 3 4	③2 3 4	④2 3 4	⑤2 3 4	⑥2 3 4
chord	C	C	C	C	F	F
words	See you later, alli-gator.	After a while, croco-	dile.	See you later, alli-	gator.	After a while, croco-

count	⑦2 3 4	⑧2 3 4	⑨2 3 4	⑩2 3 4	⑪2 3 4	⑫2 3 4
chord	C	C	G	G	C	C
words	dile.	Can't you see you're in my	way now?	Don't you know you cramp my	style?	See you later, alligator.

On the original 78 rpm record the chord pattern shown in the diagram is repeated eight times, with the guitar and saxophone playing a different tune the fifth time through. As in all rock 'n' roll, the band plays loudly, and each beat is made very clear, with strong accents on every other one: 1 <u>2</u> 3 <u>4</u>. Bill Haley's voice sounds a bit as if he's pinching his nose—a style of singing which was common in rock 'n' roll. The instruments of rock 'n' roll included **string bass, acoustic guitar, saxophone, piano** and **drums,** all of which, with **electric guitars,** would be played through loudspeakers.

Questions

1 Who were the first stars of rock 'n' roll?
2 Where did rock 'n' roll come from?
3 What were the ingredients that went into rock 'n' roll?
4 Which star 'screamed and screamed and screamed'?

Project

Look at the diagram of *See you later, alligator*. Three chords are used, **C**, **F** and **G**. Using **xylophones** and **glockenspiels** play the notes **C e g** upwards one after another for the chord of **C**, for **F** play **F a c**, and for **G** play **G b d**. Now have a go at playing the chord sequence shown in the diagram, arranging parts for the instruments like this:

count	①2 3 4	②2 3 4	③2 3 4	④2 3 4	⑤2 3 4	⑥2 3 4
xylophones	C e g	C e g	C e g	C e g	F a c	F a c
glockenspiels	C C C C	C C C C	C C C C	C C C C	F F F F	F F F F

count	⑦2 3 4	⑧2 3 4	⑨2 3 4	⑩2 3 4	⑪2 3 4	⑫2 3 4
xylophones	C e g	C e g	G b d	G b d	C e g	C e g
glockenspiels	C C C C	C C C C	G G G G	G G G G	C C C C	C C C C

After practising this, perhaps you could add some simple parts for untuned percussion instruments—**drum** and **shaker**, for example. Ask your drummer to play the beat (or count of 4) and the shaker to play some faster notes, like this:

written	♩ ♩ ♩ ♩	
drummer count	1 2 3 4	} play 12 times
shaker count	1 2 and 3 4 and	
written	♩ ♫ ♩ ♫	

From rock 'n' roll to the Beatles

Although rock 'n' roll was very popular with young people for a time it did lose much of its excitement after a couple of years. **Tommy Steele** was at first thought to be England's answer to Elvis. He started out in 1956 and began by imitating those lively songs which had caused riots in the cinemas when rock 'n' roll films had been shown. But soon his style became gentler. By 1958 he was performing songs that were not so different in style from the music the older generation enjoyed:

> As it turned out, he was natural showbiz . . . He had instant charm going for him, he was photographed with his mother and he kept right on flashing that bottomless grin . . . So he moved on from rock as fast as he could and turned to ballads, comic recitations, novelties.
>
> N. COHN *Pop from the beginning*

When Elvis joined the army in 1958, some people wondered if rock 'n' roll had been nothing more than a storm in a tea-cup. Of course you could still hear rock 'n' roll songs in the Top Thirty from stars like Pat Boone and Cliff Richard. But these were watered-down versions, with the noise and drive taken out so that they would please as many people as possible.

Tommy Steele

Cliff Richard

Pat Boone

Rhythm 'n' blues

More important for the future of pop music were two things which happened during the late 1950s in Britain (rather than in America, which had produced rock 'n' roll). The first of these was that young musicians interested in rock 'n' roll had begun to think about where it had come from. They began listening to *rhythm 'n' blues* music, which had, until the 1950s, always been played by black people in the cities of America. In Britain, white musicians set up rhythm 'n' blues bands and tried to sound as much like Howlin' Wolf and Muddy Waters as possible.

It was from this background that the famous British bands of the 1960s came. The **Rolling Stones,** for example, actually took their name from a song by Muddy Waters, and **Cream** recorded Howlin' Wolf's *Sittin' on top of the world.*

◀ Teenagers dancing rock 'n' roll in the 1950s

▼ Cream were very interested in the rhythm 'n' blues music of Howlin' Wolf

Skiffle

The second thing which happened in Britain during the late 1950s was the start of a type of music called **skiffle.** Skiffle was based on the music of the Mississippi negroes during the 1920s and 1930s. It began in Britain with a record called *Rock island line,* on which **Lonnie Donegan's** country 'n' western style voice is accompanied by guitar, string bass and washboard.

Everything about skiffle was simple. It used simple words (often railroad songs or cowboy ballads). The words were sung to simple tunes against a background of simple chords. The music was played on home-made instruments—just as it had been along the Mississippi in America 60 years before. Anything that made a sound would do (tea-chest basses, dustbin lids, soup cans, combs, for example). Within a few months of *Rock island line* coming out there were thousands of skiffle groups and clubs in Britain.

Like rock 'n' roll, the skiffle craze soon died out. What was important was that many of the pop musicians of the 1960s had their first playing experience in skiffle bands.

◀ Lonnie Donegan

Questions

1. Which British pop star was thought at first to be Britain's answer to Elvis Presley? What happened to him?
2. Which famous band took their name from a song by Muddy Waters?
3. What was skiffle?

Project

Skiffle musicians used home-made instruments. Here are some ideas about instruments you could make:

1. **Broomstick rattle**
   You will need:
   1 broomstick, as many metal bottle tops as you can get, a thin nail (about 1 in.) for each top.
   What you do:
   Remove the cork or cardboard lining from the bottle tops and drill or punch a hole through the centre of each. Nail the tops loosely to the broomstick and shake.

2. **Tin tom-tom**
   You will need:
   1 round empty coffee tin, strong wrapping paper, string or a strong rubber band.
   What you do:
   Remove the lid of the tin and cut two circles of wrapping paper each 5 cm (2 in.) larger in diameter than the mouth of the tin. Glue the two pieces of wrapping paper together and, once the glue has set, stretch the double layer of paper tightly over the mouth of the tin and fasten it firmly in place with the string or rubber band around the circumference of the tin. Play the drum lightly with a pencil or your fingertips.

3 Washtub bass

You will need:

A large washtub or pail, a broomstick, a length of thin clothes-line, an eye screw, two washers and a nut.

What you do:

Turn your washtub or pail upside down. In the centre of it drill a hole big enough to take the eye screw. Thread a washer on to the screw and push the screw into the hole you've made with the eye uppermost. Place the other washer and nut on the screw inside the tub and tighten the nut until the eye screw is really tightly in place.

Next, saw a 1.25 cm ($\frac{1}{2}$ in.) long notch in the end of the broomstick. Make it wide enough for the stick to fit over the lip of the bottom of the tub or pail. (It would be a good idea to bind the broomstick with string just above the notch so that it doesn't split.) Drill a hole near the opposite end of the broomstick big enough to take the clothes-line.

Tie one end of the line to the eye of the screw and thread the other end through the hole you've just drilled in the broomstick. Then fit the notch over the lip of the tub and hold the stick upright. Stretch the clothes-line tight and tie a knot in it on the opposite side of the stick to the eye screw.

To play the washtub bass you should pluck the clothes-line with your right hand and change notes with your left.

The lower the note the more upright the stick will be, the higher the note the more you will need to tilt the stick in towards the centre of the tub. As the string gets looser you will need to move your hand down it and press it firmly against the broomstick. It's best to wear a glove on your left hand so that it doesn't get burnt by the rope as you move it up and down.

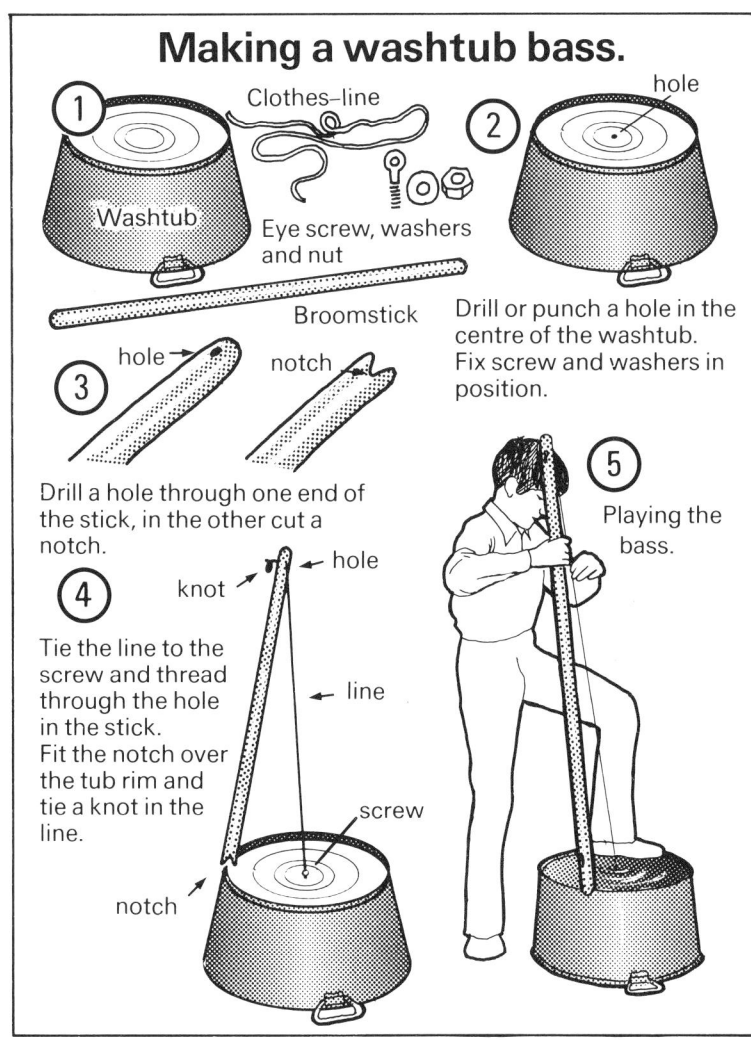

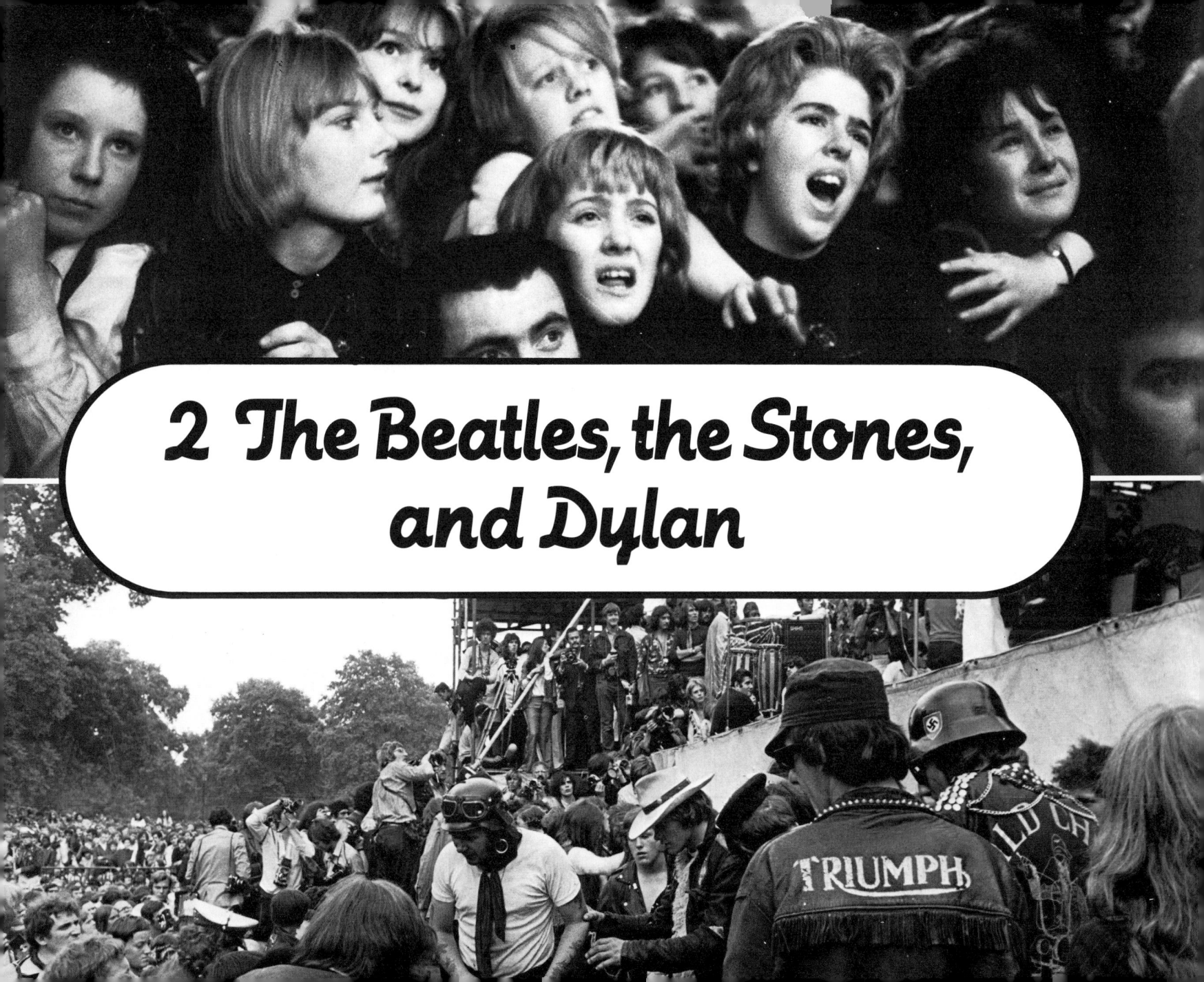

2 The Beatles, the Stones, and Dylan

The Beatles

Everyone's heard of the Beatles. But have you ever heard of the **Quarrymen**? The Quarrymen was one of the hundreds of rock 'n' roll bands in Liverpool during 1956. Playing in the band, as it toured the church halls and small clubs in the city, were two as yet unknown musicians called **Paul McCartney** and **John Lennon**. The Quarrymen didn't last long as a band. But, by 1960, Paul and John had been joined by George Harrison, and they had formed a new group called the **Silver Beatles**. In the same year they went to Hamburg, in Germany, to play at night clubs there. They returned to Liverpool in 1962.

Once back, the **Beatles,** as they were now called, played at Liverpool's most famous club, the Cavern. The crowds loved them, and they had, by now, a manager, Brian Epstein, who was getting them known outside Liverpool as well. On 6 June 1962 they were given an audition at the EMI studios in London, but were asked to change their drummer, Pete Best. Once Ringo Starr had taken over from Pete Best, the Beatles were complete. They were soon to become perhaps the most famous pop group ever.

Early days. The Beatles playing at the Cavern Club, Liverpool

The Beatles live!

Early influences

The Beatles' early songs were based on the styles of music which had helped to make rock 'n' roll: **rhythm 'n' blues** and **country 'n' western**. Their songs had the loudness and life of rhythm 'n' blues, together with the simple shape and tunes of country 'n' western. A third influence came from English **folk music**. It was this which, mixed with things from rhythm 'n' blues and country 'n' western, made the Beatles' songs sound so different. Growing up in Liverpool was important too, for here it was possible to hear each of these musical ingredients. As John Lennon said:

> 'It's where the sailors would come home with the blues records from America on the ships. I heard country 'n' western music in Liverpool before I heard rock 'n' roll . . . There were established folk, blues and country 'n' western clubs in Liverpool before rock 'n' roll . . .'

'The world's top group'

The Beatles' first record was *Love me do.* It reached number 17 in the Top Thirty at the end of 1962. This was followed by *Please please me,* which was more successful and really started Beatlemania.

Within a few months the Beatles' music had become known to millions throughout the world. During 1963 they had a record at the top of the British hit parade for 37 out of the 52 weeks. They were voted the world's top group by readers of the *New Musical Express.*

Change of style

During 1965 and 1966 the Beatles travelled a great deal. They gave concerts throughout Britain, in America, and in Europe. In 1966—the year when they had the fewest Top Thirty hits since 1963—their songs began to change in style. In *Paperback writer* and *Eleanor Rigby* the words are more thoughtful than in many of their earlier songs, and the group are interested in using new musical ideas, and new sorts of sounds, to help get the meaning of the words across.

Eleanor Rigby is about a woman who lives alone and dreams about how different her life might have been if things had worked out better. She picks up the rice after someone else's wedding, and won't let anyone know how lonely she is. To get these ideas over, the Beatles use violins and a cello to accompany Paul's sad, folk-style song.

Loneliness was also the theme of the Beatles' most famous album—*Sergeant Pepper's lonely hearts' club band*—which came out in 1967. This album was new in pop music because of the way in which most of the songs were concerned with the same basic idea (of loneliness). Sergeant Pepper's band was there to cheer up the lonely people.

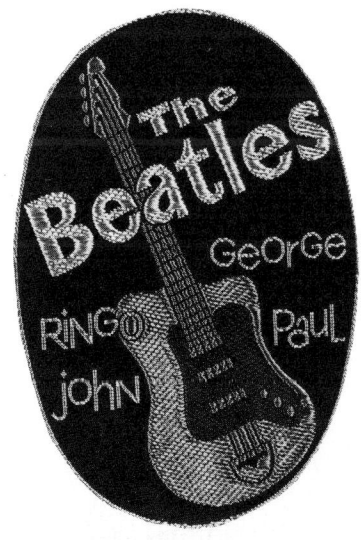

The end

During 1968 the Beatles visited India, and then returned to make their last three albums together: *The Beatles, Abbey Road* and *Let it be.* One of the tracks on *The Beatles, Revolution 9,* is rather like some pieces by modern classical composers. All sorts of sounds—car horns, shouts, musical instruments, radio programmes—are put together to make a sort of *sound picture,* rather as you might put colours together if you were a painter.

Abbey Road, in London, is the address of the EMI recording studio where the group had spent so many weeks together. (See also page 44.) It was a good title for what was really their last album, and the last track on it is called *The end. Let it be* contained songs from the film with the same title, most of which they had recorded well before the album came out.

George Harrison playing the sitar ▶

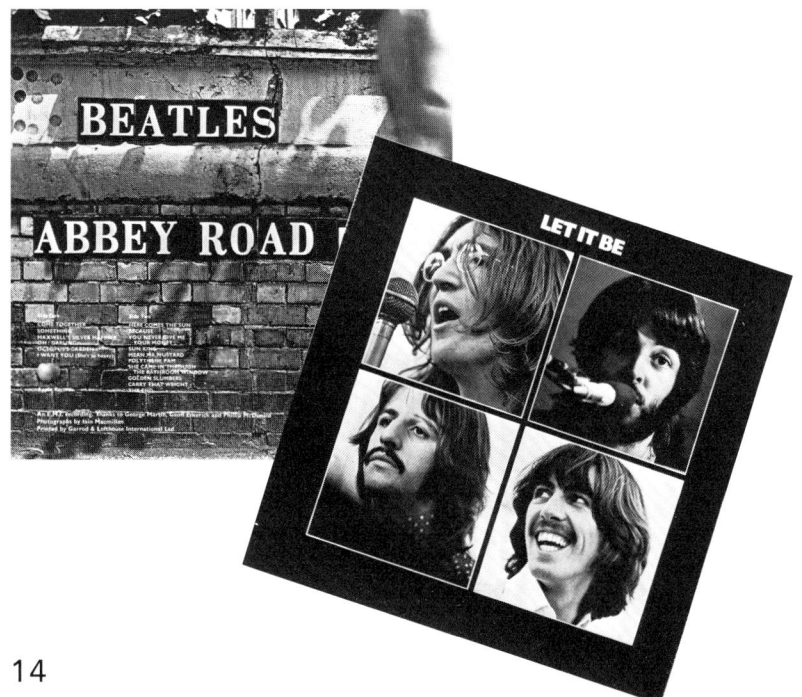

The Beatles were very important for pop music. They helped to make the words, tunes and harmonies of pop more varied and thoughtful than they had been before; and they brought into pop all sorts of new ideas—like the string players in *Eleanor Rigby*, or the sound pictures in *Revolution 9*, instruments and effects from Indian music. These all helped to make pop the wide-ranging sort of music it is today. Many of the old-style performers and record producers began to get worried during the 1960s, as the Beatles changed the course of pop music. The American record producer, Bert Berns, had a point when he said in 1966: 'These boys have genius. They'll be the ruin of us all.'

Questions

1. What were the early musical influences on the Beatles?
2. Why was Liverpool a good place for the Beatles to live?
3. What was the Beatles' first record?
4. Who was Eleanor Rigby?
5. What was the Beatles' most famous album, and what was new about it when it first came out?

Project

The Beatles' song *Get back* uses two of the chords that we came across in our rock 'n' roll project: the chords of **G** and **C** (see page 6). Using **xylophones** and **glockenspiels**, play the notes **G b** and **d** upwards for the chord of **G**, and for **C** move three steps *higher* and play **C e g**. Once you've tried the chords out a few times you'll then be able to play the chord sequence of *Get back*. Here it is with parts arranged for xylophones and glockenspiels:

count	①2 3 4	②2 3 4	③2 3 4	④2 3 4
xylophones	G b d b	G b d b	C e g C	G b d b
glockenspiels	G G G G	G G G G	C C C C	G G G G

count	⑤2 3 4	⑥2 3 4	⑦2 3 4	⑧2 3 4
xylophones	G b d b	G b d b	C e g C	G b d
glockenspiels	G G G G	G G G G	C C C C	G G G

} play the whole chord sequence twice for a complete verse of the song.

After practising the chord sequence why not try adding the tune of *Get back,* played perhaps on melodica or piano. Here it is written out in notation (the letters above the stave are the names of the chords):

(The Beatles' *Get back* is on their *Let it be* album if you would like to listen to the original.)

The Rolling Stones

The success of the Beatles' music in America made young people there interested in other British groups. The **Dave Clark Five's** *Glad all over* became a number 1 best-seller in 1964, and the **Animals,** led by Eric Burdon, were popular, too. What was unusual about British pop music at this time was that it no longer simply copied what was going on across the Atlantic. For the first time British musicians were teaching the Americans a thing or two—and, after the Beatles, it was the **Rolling Stones** who did most of the teaching.

The Stones were as different from the Beatles as could be. On stage they looked moody and fierce. Their music was strongly based on rhythm 'n' blues: loud and with a strong beat, 'frantic guitars and drums, wild vocals, bumps, grinds and twitches'. When someone described the Stones as 'the group parents hate most' they were right. When parents saw the lead singer of the Stones, **Mick Jagger,** dancing and jumping his way through a song they didn't like him—which was exactly what he wanted.

▼ The Rolling StonesMick Jagger ▶

Britain as a centre of pop music

The Rolling Stones' singles *Satisfaction* and *Get off my cloud* were typical of their style. Their album *Aftermath* became famous for its no-nonsense words and music. Later, in *Their satanic majesties' request,* produced at the same time as the Beatles' *Sergeant Pepper* album, they used electronic studio effects and their music lost some of its drive and vigour. In *Beggar's banquet,* released later, they returned to their earlier rhythm 'n' blues based style, which pleased their fans.

It was the difference between the Beatles and the Rolling Stones which was important for British pop music. The Beatles showed that pop could be influenced by other forms of music and that it could be serious and thoughtful in a way which people had earlier thought only classical music could be. The Rolling Stones, on the other hand, showed how it was possible to take the ingredients of only one style, rhythm 'n' blues, and make them into a new and original kind of music which had much of the excitement of early rock 'n' roll.

Between them, the Beatles and the Stones helped make Britain equal to America as a centre of pop music.

Questions

1 Which group had a hit record with *Glad all over?*
2 What were the main differences, musical and otherwise, between the Rolling Stones and the Beatles?

Project

Collect all the information you can about the Rolling Stones and the Beatles and then put together folders of information (in your own words) and pictures of the two groups.

Bob Dylan

At about the time the Silver Beatles began playing in Liverpool, England, **Bob Dylan** arrived in New York. Dylan was from the northern American state of Minnesota. He had spent much time while at school listening to the music of Hank Williams, a country 'n' western star. There were two main reasons for his visit to New York. The first was that he wanted to meet his new idol, folk-singer Woody Guthrie. The second was that he wanted to try out his own songs in the coffee bars and folk clubs of Greenwich Village.

One of the first people to hear him was Joan Baez, already well known as a folk singer there. She was impressed: 'He knocked me out completely . . . He was just astounding . . .' But what was it about Bob Dylan's style that made him so special?

First, his voice, which, although influenced by the country 'n' western nose-pinching sound of Hank Williams, was the sort of voice you couldn't mistake for anyone else's. Second, like Woody Guthrie, Dylan *talked* his songs as much as he sang them—and because of this he was able to make the words clear. Dylan, like other folk singers, accompanied himself on the acoustic guitar; but the third thing which made him rather special was his choice of themes for his songs, and the poetry he invented to put these themes across to his audiences.

Protest

Instead of writing about things which had happened in the past, Bob Dylan chose to bring folk music into the present. He wrote songs about the issues which were concerning young people at the time. These included civil rights and nuclear war. This new sort of music came to be called **protest music.** A song that

Bob Dylan ▶

Dylan wrote in 1962, *Blowin' in the wind*, had become so popular by the following year that it was called the civil rights anthem. The song came out on his second album *Freewheelin' Bob Dylan* and was sung at many civil rights rallies and marches.

At the time of the Cuba missile crisis in 1962 Dylan wrote another song which soon became famous: *A hard rain's gonna fall*. There had almost been a war over the missiles and the words of the song are a warning of the destruction that might have happened:

I met a young child beside a dead pony,
I met a white man who walked a black dog,
I met a young woman whose body was burning,
I met a young girl, she gave me a rainbow . . .
And it's a hard, it's a hard, it's a hard, and it's a hard,
It's a hard rain's a-gonna fall.

By taking themes like this and singing about them in his own special way, Bob Dylan soon became world-famous.

▲ New style Dylan with electric guitar and backing group

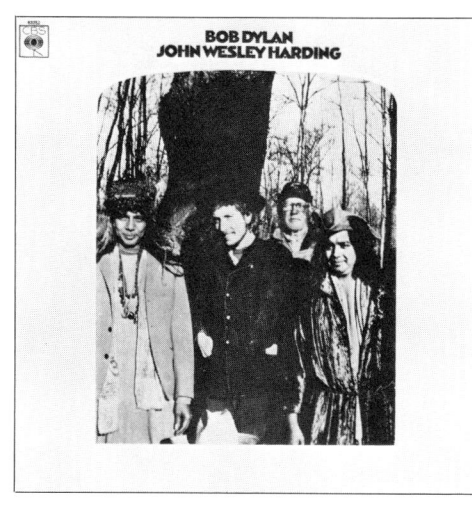

The John Wesley Harding album.
Dylan is second from left.

Dylan and the Beatles

Dylan's tour of Britain in 1964 was a great success. It was also very important for the future of pop music, because he and the Beatles met and influenced each other's music a great deal. He was impressed by the cleverness of their tunes and harmonies, and they showed interest in his themes of protest and his colourful poetry.

Once back in America Dylan changed his style. Instead of using only the acoustic guitar as accompaniment he began using backing musicians and electric instruments. His songs became more influenced by the sounds of the Beatles and other British groups. As a result his album *Bringing it all back home* was one of his most popular yet and the single *Like a rolling stone* soon became a best-seller. Later, in 1967, Bob Dylan returned to something more like his original style in the album *John Wesley Harding*. He had shown that folk and pop were no longer separate forms of music.

Questions

1. What was special about Bob Dylan's style of music?
2. What was protest music?
3. What did Dylan and the Beatles learn from each other?

Project

Listen to Dylan's song *The Ballad of Frankie Lee and Judas Priest* from his *John Wesley Harding* album and see if you can hear how the tune is made up of only four notes and how there are only three different chords used in the accompaniment. The notes that are used are **C, b, a** and **g,** and the chords that go with these notes are **C (C, e, g), E minor (E, g, b)** and **D minor (D, f, a).** Here's the tune written out to the words of the first verse. Your job is to sing and/or play it, and then once you've practised it, you should try adding the accompaniment. The chords are shown above the tune and lower down the page you'll find a suggestion as to how to play them on xylophones and glockenspiels:

Folk rock

When Bob Dylan performed at the Newport Folk Festival in 1965 he brought together folk and pop music by singing folk-style songs to the accompaniment of pop-style amplified instruments. This new way of presenting folk material came to be called **folk-rock**.

One of the style's first hits was the **Byrd's** version of Dylan's *Mr Tambourine Man*. Like Dylan, the Byrds owed much to country 'n' western music. Their voices had that typical nose-pinching sound, they used acoustic guitars a great deal, and their songs were clear-cut in shape and tuneful. Other folk-rock groups included the **Lovin' Spoonful**, the **Mamas and Papas**, and, perhaps the most famous of all, **Simon and Garfunkel**, with their *Sound of silence* and *Mrs Robinson*.

▼ Folk-rock: Simon and Garfunkel

Questions

1 What was folk-rock?
2 How did folk-rock come about?

Project

Listen to the two different versions of *Mr Tambourine Man* made by Bob Dylan (on his *Bringing it all back home* album) and by the Byrds (on their *Mr Tambourine Man* album), and make a list of the differences between the two. What instruments are used? Is the song sung differently? Which performance do you prefer?

The West Coast sound

Folk-rock was the first new style which had appeared in America for some years. It was soon followed by what became called the **West Coast sound.** California was the centre of this style, and its concerts often took place at the Fillmore Hall in San Francisco. The **Beach Boys** were the first of the West Coast groups to become popular, with their single *Surfin' USA*.

Other groups, such as **Grateful Dead, Country Joe and the Fish** and **Captain Beefheart and his Magic Band,** played music which was better suited to album release than single. Their performances made use of many special effects, both musical and otherwise. Loud screeching noises (called **feedback**, and caused by playing electric instruments in a direct line with their loudspeakers), heavy repeated tunes in the bass (called **riffs**) and long guitar solos were accompanied by fantastic light-shows, films and dancers on stage.

Many young people were critical of the American way of life at this time, and their feelings were summed up in the words, ideas and music of **Frank Zappa** with his band the Mothers of Invention. Zappa was strongly influenced by classical music, and orchestral sounds and other ideas from this form of music (see page 29) are added to the many other effects to be heard on their albums *Freak out* and *Absolutely free*.

Questions

1 Which group first became popular with *Surfin' USA*?
2 What special effects, musical and otherwise, were to be found in performances by West Coast groups?

◀ The Beach Boys taking time off in Hyde Park, London

Pop in 1967

By 1967 pop had come a long way since the days of Bill Haley's *Shake, rattle and roll.* In Britain the Beatles had shown that it could be varied and thoughtful and the Rolling Stones had proved that rhythm 'n' blues could form the basis of a new musical style. In America Bob Dylan had shown that pop music could be concerned with serious issues and folk-rock and West Coast rock had come into being. Then, in 1967, two things happened. Together they summed up many of these developments, and showed the way in which pop music— American and British—was to go in the future.

The Monterey Festival

The first of these happenings was the **Monterey Pop Music Festival.** Monterey is a town on the West coast of America. To it in June 1967 came thousands of young people intent on hearing the music of amongst others, **Jimi Hendrix,** the **Who, Simon and Garfunkel, Otis Redding** and **Ravi Shankar.** What was interesting about Monterey was the range of music covered. For example, if you compare the music of Hendrix and the Who with that of Simon and Garfunkel you'll find that they are very different. The Who were even livelier performers than the Rolling Stones:

> Always, they were murderous: Pete Townshend used to smash his guitar full into the amps, shattering it like kindling, and the amps would scream out feedback, would squeal and explode. And Roger Daltrey who sang, used to swing his mike like a lariat and crash it against the drums, and Keith Moon used to play drums with twenty arms, mouth gaping and eyes bugged, flailing and thrashing like some dervish . . .
>
> N. COHN *Pop from the beginning*

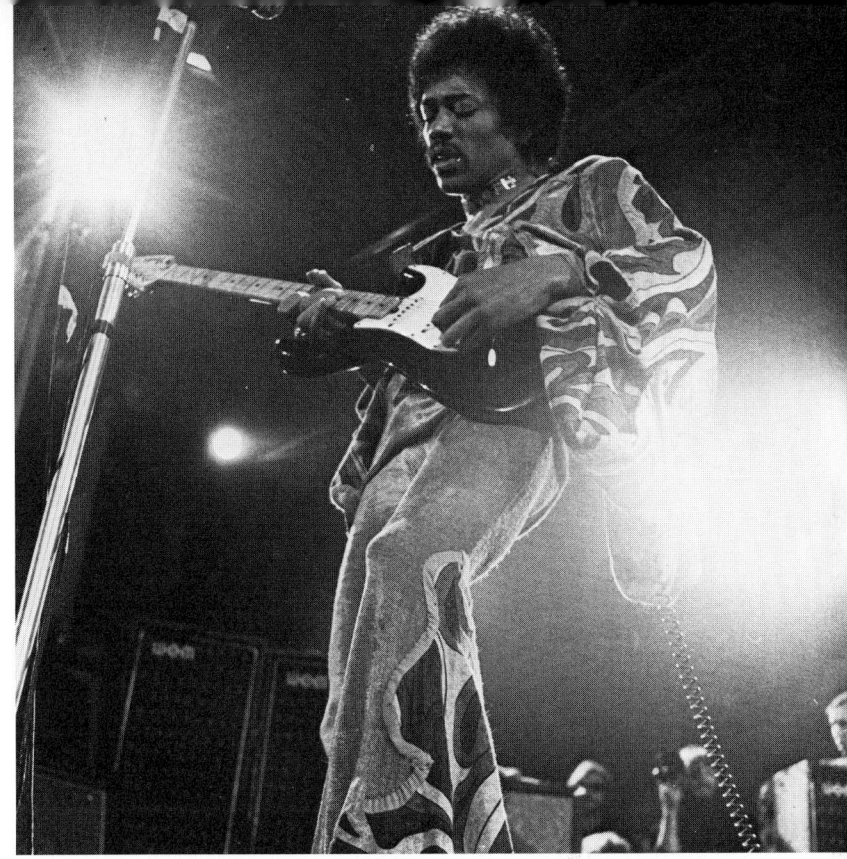

▲ Jimi Hendrix, master of the electric guitar ▼ At the Hyde Park concert, 1969

▲ The Who

The Who's music, like that of Hendrix, was loud and aggressive, played on electric instruments and with a strong beat from drums. Simon and Garfunkel were quieter altogether. Their style was folk-rock, they used acoustic instruments a great deal, and they were not interested in a heavy beat. Yet, although the styles of the Who and Simon and Garfunkel were so different they played to the same audience at Monterey.

Ravi Shankar was an Indian musician whose playing could hardly be a greater contrast.

The important thing which Monterey showed was that pop music now had many different styles and interests, and that these could all exist at the same time, could form part of the same festival. In 1955 if you liked pop music there wasn't any choice. It was rock 'n' roll or nothing. Twelve years later you could like rhythm 'n' blues or folk or Indian music. They were now all a part of pop music, with many other styles.

Super albums

The second important thing which happened in 1967 was that the most famous groups produced long playing records which became called **super albums**. This was because the records contained so many studio effects, some electronic, some orchestral, some from Indian music. They took longer to make and, of course, cost very much more than in the past. The best known super albums were the Beatles' *Sergeant Pepper's lonely hearts' club band*, the Rolling Stones' *Their satanic majesties' request*, and a record by the Beach Boys, called *Smiley smile*.

The Beatles' first album—*Please please me*—had taken one day, and cost £400 to make; *Sergeant Pepper* took four months, and cost £25,000. Hunter Davies, in his biography of the group, gives some reasons for this change:

> At one time their songs were recorded at one go and on one track or at the most two. Now it takes at least four tracks as they continually think of another instrument or effects to add. And when a forty-piece orchestra is used, as in *A day in the life* (on *Sergeant Pepper*), the expense is enormous.
>
> H. DAVIES *The Beatles* Heinemann

The first track on the Beach Boys' album *Smiley smile* cost about £15,000 and one song alone, *Good vibrations*, was the result of six months' work in the studio. During this time 400,000 feet (or 90 hours) of magnetic tape were used to make the three minute, 35 second master tape.

It is unusual nowadays to find so many studio effects packed into one record. Tastes have changed. But the super albums showed just what could be done, and since then **studio effects** and **orchestral instruments** have remained an important part of pop. This means, of course, that there will often be important differences between live and recorded versions of a particular song.

Questions

1. What were the two things which made 1967 such an important year in the history of pop music?
2. What kind of music does Ravi Shankar play?

Projects

Listen carefully to the Beatles' *Sergeant Pepper* album and see if you can hear the effects that are listed:

1 *Sergeant Pepper's lonely hearts' club band* (side 1 version)
    a Audience noise including chattering, applause and screaming
    b Instruments tuning up
    c Brass instruments playing

2 *Within you, without you* (side 2)
    a Indian musical instruments including sitar (a string instrument) and tabla (a drum)

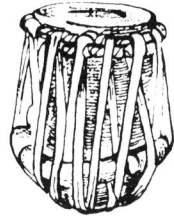
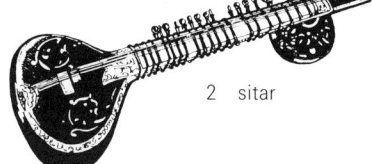

Indian musical instruments used in the Beatles' song *Within you, without you.*

1 tabla   2 sitar

    b Scooping voice
    c Violin played with a bow and also plucked
    d Laughter

3 *Good morning, Good morning* (side 2)
    a Distorted sounds of guitars, chorus and brass instruments
    b Use of echo
    c Animals and birds including a cockerel, dog, horse and sheep
    d The sound of the hunt including hounds and huntsman's bugle

If you have time then listen to the whole album and see if you can make out the sounds of the following classical music instruments and groups: string quartet, harp, clarinet, harpsichord and piano.

After 1967

After the Monterey Festival of 1967 other large-scale festivals took place. Perhaps the most famous of all was **Woodstock,** in 1969. The festivals continued to include many of the different styles of pop in the same concert. And because those styles still exist in the 1980s, the idea of pop music becoming 'out of date' is much less important. Today, people still listen to the records of, for example, Cream, a band which broke up in the late 1960s. They have not dated at all. Pink Floyd's album *Saucerful of secrets* came out in 1968. It is different from their later albums but not out-of-date.

    We need to remember, too, many groups and artists still go on working. Pink Floyd still exists as a group. Soft Machine, the Rolling Stones, Bob Dylan, and members of the Beatles who were playing in 1967 are still recording over ten years later. Some people say that this has made pop music dull and unexciting. Others say that because musicians are not trying to do something new just for the sake of it their compositions have become more thoughtful.

Questions

1 Which famous pop festival took place in 1969?
2 Name some pop musicians from today who were playing in 1967.

3 The influences on pop

Pop and jazz

The rhythm 'n' blues influence on rock 'n' roll was the first of a number of important things which **jazz** has given to pop. The **twelve-bar blues**, which formed the basis of rock 'n' roll, has since been used in many different ways by pop musicians. Have you ever heard the blues and wondered how it sounded so sad? Well, important in helping the blues to sound so unhappy is the way in which singers slide certain notes in and out of tune, slowly and on purpose. Many pop musicians have used these blue note slides both in their singing and guitar playing.

Another thing which jazz musicians gave to pop was the idea of having a percussion player. The beat in pop is 'laid down' by the drummer. The speed of the song depends on him, and when there's an instrumental solo it's the drummer's job to hold things together. As well as drums, he plays tom-toms, cymbals, cowbells and a number of other instruments.

▼ These jazz musicians play trumpet (centre) and saxophones

Riffs

Jazz also gave pop musicians the idea of using **riffs**. These are short tunes or groups of chords which are played over and over again to form the basis of a song or an instrumental solo.

In classical music this is called an **ostinato**. But pop differs from classical music in the way in which riffs are used. In pop it doesn't matter how obvious the riff is. Sometimes it's enough for the pattern to be repeated with nothing much else happening (as at the end of the Beatles' *Hey Jude*). In classical music the composer tries his hardest to cover up the ostinato, to paper over the cracks so that the joins don't show.

Another thing which has come into pop from jazz is **improvisation**. Unlike at classical concerts, in pop and jazz performances there are always opportunities for musicians to make up their own tunes over a riff or chord sequence. This is, of course, one of the things that make live concerts so exciting.

Questions

1   What musical things has pop taken from jazz?
2   What is improvisation?

Project

Using any instruments that you can find (xylophones, glockenspiels, melodicas, recorders, piano) try playing each of these riffs:

When you've practised each one separately divide your players into two groups and play both riffs together.

Pop and folk music

Pop took from folk music the use of certain scales called **modes**. The mode you choose gives your song its basic melody and chords. You can easily find what modes are by playing the white notes only of the piano keyboard. For example, if you pick the note D and then play upwards until you come to the next D, you will have played the D (or **Dorian**) mode. If you then choose the note E, and play upwards until the next E, that is the E (or **Phrygian**) mode. You'll notice that, although you have played basically the same notes in each case, the pattern of large steps (**tones**) and small steps (**semi-tones**) changes according to the note you start on. (On the piano keyboard white notes with black notes between them form large steps.)

Other modes which pop and folk musicians use in their composing are the **C, G** and **A**. Here they all are written out:

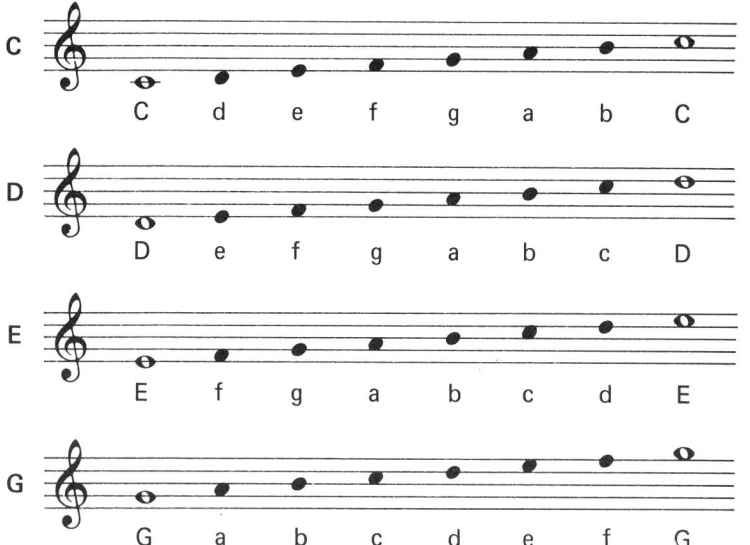

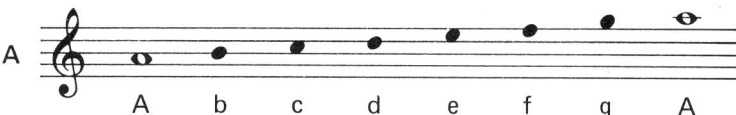

There are many examples in pop music of tunes which are completely in one of the modes. One of the Beatles' earliest songs, *I feel fine* was in the G mode, while Bob Dylan's famous *All along the watchtower,* Carly Simon's *You're so vain* and Bob Marley's *I shot the sheriff* are in the A mode.

Questions

1   What musical things has pop taken from folk?
2   What is meant by a *mode*?

Project

Play the D mode going upwards on a xylophone or piano:

count	① 2 3 4	② 2 3 4
play	D e f g	a b c D

Then try out the E, G and A modes in turn. Finally choose one of these modes and make up a tune of your own using it. Remember to start and stop on the note which gives the mode its name.

Pop and classical music

Dave Hill of Slade once gave an interview during which he said how much he liked classical music. The same is true of other pop musicians; in fact there are many examples of pop musicians taking ideas from classical music and putting them into their own music. During the 1960s Procul Harum's *Whiter shade of pale* and the Beatles' *You never give me your money* were two songs in which the composers took 18th century chord sequences and made them part of pop. Other groups, like Yes and Pink Floyd, have continued the idea of using classical-style harmonies.

Some musicians have gone even further and actually re-arranged classical pieces for pop instruments. On Yes' *Fragile* album Rick Wakeman has arranged the third movement of Brahms' Fourth Symphony for keyboard instruments (and, using multi-track tape-recorder, he plays all the parts himself!). Manfred Mann's *Joybringer* was an arrangement of part of Holst's *Planets' Suite*. Rod Argent's arrangement of Satie's *Gymnopédie No. 1* also became popular. And in 1981 the Royal Philharmonic Orchestra's *Hooked on classics* was a Top Thirty hit. This contained tunes by Grieg, Handel and Mozart.

Classical instruments

Another thing which pop musicians have done is taken classical music instruments and made them firmly a part of pop. The string players in the Beatles' *Eleanor Rigby* and the symphony orchestra on the *Abbey Road* album are examples from the 1960s. More recently **Rod Stewart** used strings in his *I don't want to talk about it* and **Emerson, Lake and Palmer's** arrangement of Copland's *Fanfare for the common man* uses brass instruments and kettledrums.

▲ Gustav Holst

▲ Manfred Mann recorded a version of part of Gustav Holst's *Jupiter* which became a Top Thirty hit

Questions

1. What musical things has pop taken from classical music?
2. Which classical music instruments are used in Emerson, Lake and Palmer's *Fanfare for the common man*?

Project

Manfred Mann's *Joybringer* is an arrangement of the tune from *Jupiter*, a movement from the classical composer Gustav Holst's suite *The Planets*. Listen to the classical and pop versions of the tune and think about the differences between them. What instruments are used in each? Is one version more lively than the other? Which do you prefer?

In the same way as Manfred Mann, Emerson, Lake and Palmer took ideas from classical music when they decided to record a version of Aaron Copland's *Fanfare for the common man*. Listen to the two versions. If you were Aaron Copland would you like what had been done to your music? Pretend you are the composer and write a letter to the pop group saying what you think.

Pop and electronic music

The German composer Stockhausen was one of the first to 'write' electronic music in the early 1950s. It soon became an important part of modern classical music. Like pop, electronic music is *meant* to be heard through loudspeakers, and it was not surprising that pop musicians soon began to see the possibilities of using electronic effects in their music.

We are used to hearing electronic effects as background sounds in radio, television and films. A few seconds worth of strange echoing sounds are enough to make us think of journeys into space, and electronic sounds are often used to create feelings of sadness, creepiness, violence and so on.

Feedback

The simplest way of producing such effects is by causing **feedback**. Anyone who has been to a pop concert will have heard those screeching noises which sometimes result when amplifiers are tested, and instruments moved across the stage. These noises are caused when a microphone or instrumental pick-up (see page 40) hears *itself* through its own loudspeaker. In order to cause this as part of his playing, an electric guitarist simply needs to stand in a direct line with the speaker to which his instrument is connected. Once the screeching starts it can be affected by the player moving his guitar from side to side and up

This electronic music studio has the latest equipment. It uses computers as well as synthesizers and multi-track tape recorders in the recording process. Studios like this prepare pre-recorded tapes for pop groups such as Soft Machine and Tangerine Dream to use in their electronic compositions.

Here is a description of how a recording is made:
The sound of a voice or an instrument is fed into the computer via a microphone (**A**).
The computer (**B**) analyses the sound and stores the results on a magnetic data tape (**C**).
The computer processes the results to make the required sounds (**D**). (The central control panel for the computer is at **E**.)
Next, the sound is passed through a synthesizer (**F**) where reverberation and filtering effects may be added.
Finally, the sound is recorded on an ordinary reel-to-reel tape recorder (**G**).
The machine marked **H** has four separate channels for multi-tracking, that is, four different recordings can be superimposed.

and down, and made louder if he moves closer to the speaker. The **Jimi Hendrix Experience** and the **Who** were two bands who used feedback a great deal.

However, feedback is a limited means of causing electronic sounds. Pop groups whose interests lie in electronic compositions and not merely effects will use pre-recorded tapes and a synthesizer (see page 41) as well as their electric instruments. One of the most famous of such bands is **Pink Floyd** and the complex equipment which they use on stage gives some idea of the ambitious nature of their music. **Tangerine Dream** and **Soft Machine** have also composed electronic pieces.

Questions

1 What is feedback and how is it caused?
2 What is a synthesizer?

Project

Listen to the Beatles' *Revolution 9* (on the White Album) and John Cage's *Fontana Mix*. These two pieces are collages of sounds—sounds of different sorts, some electronic, some made by musical instruments, some from everyday life. All of these are mingled or contrasted with each other in the same way as a painter mingles or contrasts colours in an art collage. Using a cassette recorder make up some sound collages of your own. It would help if you thought of a particular idea, like *Street music*. Take the recorder into your nearest village or town and record the sounds you hear—traffic, church bells, a radio programme heard through an open window, and so on. Back in school, with the help of your teacher and the use of a reel-to-reel tape recorder, you can experiment with mingling and contrasting the sounds you have already recorded with other sounds and musical ideas. Further collage suggestions: *Autumn music, Seaside music, Travel music*.

▲ Marc Bolan using feedback

4 Pop styles today: from folk to punk rock

One of the most exciting things about pop music today is its variety of styles. In this section of the book we'll take a look at the most important of these.

Hard rock

Hard rock is loud, aggressive music. It has rhythm 'n' blues as its basis. Often there will be a firm, easily remembered **bass riff** (repeated tune), which is supported by a heavy beat from drums and a simple one or two chord accompaniment from rhythm guitar or keyboard. The melodies of hard rock songs are usually simple, too. Often the most exciting things happen during the lead guitarist's solos. During these solos the other players also 'take off'; the bass gets away from simply repeating the riff, and the percussion player invents new and more complicated rhythms. This sort of music is best heard live when the solos can be longer and the players can respond to their audience. **Iron Butterfly** and **Grand Funk Railroad** are American examples of bands which play in this style, **Edgar Broughton** and **Ten Years After** British examples.

Rhythm 'n' blues

It was the famous band **Cream** which took the blues notes, voice and short riffs of rhythm 'n' blues and added the folk mode tunes and chords of British pop. Listen to their albums *Wheels of fire* and *Disraeli gears*, for example. Recent examples of bands which come into this area are the Groundhogs and the Jeff Beck Group; more famous are **Led Zeppelin** who were set up by guitarist Jimmy Page in 1968. Strongly influenced by Cream and rhythm 'n' blues in the beginning, Led Zeppelin became one of the most important and original-sounding groups of the 1970's. Listen, for example, to their double album *The song remains the same*.

Led Zeppelin ▶

Rock 'n' roll

Several bands today model their music on early **rock 'n' roll**. The difference between present-day rock 'n' roll and that of the 1950s is that the quality of amplification is now much better, and the rhythm 'n' blues influence is stronger. Rock 'n' roll bands are popular at dances and clubs as well as in the concert hall. Examples are **Showaddywaddy** and **Sha-na-na**. Rock'n'roll singer **Shakin' Stevens** has also had a number of important Top Thirty hits.

◀ Punk style—coloured hair and bicycle chains

◀ Gary Glitter

Punk rock

During 1977 a 'new wave' of **punk rock** began in Britain. In fact what is new is not so much the music, which is based on the form and three simple chords of rock 'n' roll, but the *words* of the songs which are often negative. *Pretty vacant* and *Going nowhere* are examples of songs by the **Sex Pistols** which were popular during 1977. Other punk groups are the **Stranglers** and the **Buzzcocks** with their single *Love you more.*

Commercial pop

During the 1970s there have been many performers whose songs have been extremely popular and often in the Top Thirty lists. Usually the music of these groups is a mixture of styles and yet simple enough to have instant appeal. For example, there's **Slade** whose music is cheerful and good to stamp your feet to—'good time music', as lead singer Noddy Holder once said. Slade's live performances are particularly effective, as are those of **Status Quo**, another popular band whose style is a mixture of rock 'n' roll and rhythm 'n' blues. **Mud** recorded some songs by rhythm 'n' blues star Chuck Berry on their **Mud Rock** album of 1974; as lead guitarist Rob Davis said, 'we thought we'd try and do a different sort of thing and dig up old stuff and rehash it in our own way'. The **Osmonds, Gary Glitter,** the **Bee Gees, Blondie** and **Abba** are other examples of performers who have produced enjoyable music, which has been commercially successful.

Soul

Soul is yet another form of music which was influenced by rhythm 'n' blues. It uses the electric instruments, short riffs and heavy beat of rhythm 'n' blues and combines these with the **call** (soloist) and **response** (chorus) pattern of gospel music. Well known stars during the 1960s were **Aretha Franklin** and **Otis Redding**. Since then soul has become more varied in style and is based in three American centres, Memphis, Detroit and New York. Of these, Detroit is the most famous as the home of **Tamla Motown records**. The **Supremes**, the **Jackson Five** and the **Commodores** are examples of Motown artists, as is **Stevie Wonder** whose popular album *Hotter than July* well shows the variety of style in today's soul music. Recently a number of white musicians have used soul as the basis of their style. Best known of these is the **Average White Band** with their album *Soul searching*.

▼ The Jackson Five, popular Motown stars

The Average White Band—soul musicians from Scotland
▼

Reggae

Reggae became very popular in Britain during the 1970s. Because of this *Melody Maker* now regularly publishes a list of hits. The interest in the music lies in the offbeat rhythms and bass riffs. The African sounding singing voice is also basic to reggae style. Reggae stars include **Tapper Zukie** and **Bob Marley and the Wailers**, with their album *Uprising*, the last before Marley's death in 1981. Listen out too, for **Merger**, who played at Dylan's Blackbushe concert in 1978, and **Aswad**. Recently reggae has influenced the music of some important new groups. Most famous of these are **The Police**, with their album *Reggatta de blanc*.

The Top Thirty Reggae singles list from the Melody Maker of 15 July, 1978. Notice the two appearances from Tapper Zukie

```
 1  (1)  SHE WANT A PHENSIC  Tapper Zukie, Front Line
 2  (4)  DON'T ASK MY NEIGHBOURS
                              Sheila Hylton, Island
 3  (2)  SATISFY MY SOUL
                     Bob Marley and the Wailers, Island
 4  (5)  JESUS DREAD ............... Trinity, Grove Music
 5  (3)  BLACK WOMAN ... Judy Mowatt, Grove Music
 6  (7)  BACK A YARD ............... In Crowd, Cactus
 7  (8)  WAITING IN THE PARK ... Chantells, Phase One
 8  (8)  ROCK ..................... Matumbi, Harvest
    (12) MASH DOWN ......... Roots, Greensleeves
10  (10) I LOVE MARIJUANA ... Linval Thompson, Attack
11  (—)  LAND OF THE RISING SUN
                          Dennis Reid, Greensleeves
12  (15) PRODIGAL SON ............ Steel Pulse, Island
13  (6)  PHENSIC ......... Ranking Starcky, Third World
    (18) MIDNIGHT ............... Willie Lindo, Black Wax
15  (13) JOHN PUBLIC ........ Gregory Isaacs, Hawkeye
16  (17) CAIRO ............... Joy Ella Blade, Front Line
    (18) YOU'VE HAD YOUR CHANCE
                              Joy Mack, Four Sixty
18  (—)  NEW STAR ............ Tapper Zukie, New Star
19  (13) EQUAL RIGHTS ....... Dennis Brown, Lightning
20  (—)  THAT'S WHAT FRIENDS ARE FOR
                                Janet Kay, D-Roy
Two titles tied for 8th, 13th, 16th positions.
```

Folk

By the end of the 1960s the folk-rock style, which had started with the Byrd's version of *Mr Tambourine Man,* had more or less died out. Both the Lovin' Spoonful and the Mamas and Papas broke up as groups, although the Byrds continued with several changes of musicians. You can, however, still hear something of the folk-rock influence in the music of **Paul Simon, Art Garfunkel** and the **Band,** whose music takes much from cowboy songs of the late 19th century.

Another type of folk group comes from the traditional folk-dance band, in which the violinist was always important. Such groups play traditional material but with amplified acoustic and electric instruments. They are particularly popular in Britain. **Steeleye Span**, with their albums *Storm force ten*, *Oriental masters* and *Sails of silver*, are the best known, and **Lindisfarne**, **Fairport Convention** and the **Chieftains** are other examples of bands who have played in this style.

Not all folk singers changed to folk rock with Bob Dylan in 1965. **Joan Baez** has kept to the original voice and acoustic guitar style, and, although **Donovan** and **Roy Harper** did use amplified instruments on record, for their stage performances they used acoustic guitar only. Kevin Koyne and John Martyn are more recent examples of folk singers.

Joan Baez

The solo singer

At the end of the 1960s there was an increase in the popularity of the music of **Carole King,** the American solo singer who both wrote and performed her own songs. Her album *Tapestry* became one of the best selling records ever. Probably one reason for its success was that, with the Beatles no longer existing as a group, there was a need for tuneful and well-written pop songs with serious content.

Carly Simon and **James Taylor** are further examples of American solo singers, and indeed both have worked with Carole King. In Britain there is **Elton John,** with his famous *Rocket man* and *Daniel,* and **Kate Bush** who, although very different from one another, come into this style. As in folk music, the song arrangements are carefully done so that the singer's voice and the words of the song come across clearly. The instrumental line up tends to be piano or acoustic guitar with bass guitar and some light percussion and orchestral effects.

Elton John

◀ Yes's album *Going for the One*

Progressive

Pink Floyd is thought of as a **progressive** band, although the term progressive is a difficult one to explain exactly. It certainly doesn't mean that the music of Pink Floyd is *better* than that of other bands, but that their compositions have *progressed beyond* what we expect from most pop. For example, instead of being the usual length of about three minutes Pink Floyd's songs are mostly too large in scale for anything but album release; and, instead of putting across an easily understood message, as in the case of most pop songs, the words of Pink Floyd's songs are serious and often complicated. They use classical music and other effects whenever these help to illustrate the meaning of the words and, as in the case of their double album *The wall*, there will often be a general theme for the whole record. The recording and mixing of a progressive album might well take as long as six months, because of the complexity of the music and arrangements. **Jethro Tull**, **Genesis** and **Yes**, with their album *Going for the One*, are further examples of progressive bands.

Experimental

Experimental pop musicians will often try out, or *experiment* with, new sounds and musical ideas. They are usually strongly influenced by modern jazz and electronic music. From jazz come the percussion player's complicated rhythms and the way he uses brushes on cymbals to produce delicate effects. The complicated chords, riffs and rhythms of modern jazz are also found in experimental pop. From electronic music comes the idea of playing with sounds for their own sake and regardless of any beat. **Soft Machine** and **Third Ear Band** are examples of experimental groups, and **Tangerine Dream** (see page 31), with their album *Sorcerer* have become very popular recently. Their music is more electronic than jazz influenced and involves the use of synthesizers and pre-recorded tapes. It is also very loud, played live.

Questions

Hard rock
1 What are the musical ingredients of hard rock?
2 Why is hard rock best heard live?

Rhythm 'n' blues
1 Which famous band produced the albums *Wheels of fire* and *Disraeli gears*?
2 Who is Jimmy Page?

Rock 'n' roll
1 What are the differences between today's rock 'n' roll and that of the 1950s?
2 Where are rock 'n' roll bands popular?

Punk rock
1 What is punk rock based on?
2 *Love you more* was a single by which band?

Commercial pop
1 Whose music was described as 'good time music'?
2 Rob Davis was lead guitarist with which band?

Soul
1 What are the musical ingredients of soul?
2 Which American city is the home of Tamla Motown records?

Reggae
1 Where does reggae come from?
2 Bob Marley was a reggae singer. What was the name of his band?

Folk
1 Which group was influenced by 19th century cowboy songs?
2 Which country do Steeleye Span come from?

The solo singer
1 Which album by Carole King became one of the best selling records ever?
2 Who wrote *Rocket man* and *Daniel*?

Progressive
1 Whose music can you hear on the double album *The wall*?
2 Why does the recording of a progressive album take a long time?

Experimental
1 What influences from modern jazz can be found in experimental pop?
2 Which of these is the name of an experimental group: Apple Pie, Tangerine Dream, Peach Sundae, Blackcurrant Jelly?

5 The electric band and the recording business

Amplification

From the beginning loudness has been an important part of pop music. One thing which young people particularly enjoyed about the rock 'n' roll music of Bill Haley and Elvis Presley was that it was loud enough to put older people off. With the many improvements which have been made since then in amplifying and loudspeaker equipment, it is now possible for groups to play very loudly, but without their music losing its clarity, as often happened before.

Of course, good equipment is very expensive; at certain times (an open air festival, for example) it can be so powerful that the sound can damage your hearing if you get too close to the loudspeakers. In any case, being *too* close to speakers is not a good idea, since they are designed to spread the sound and you get the best effect at a distance.

Problems of loudness

Certainly the volume of sound at any concert in a club or hall will seem great to someone not used to live music, and some groups are not skilful in judging the different needs of different shaped and sized halls. However, given good music, played on good instruments, and equipment carefully set for the building, then loudness itself can be a useful effect. For example, a set of chords, played in a straightforward way, has a feeling of breadth and depth added to it when very loud. Sound waves actually cause a disturbance in the air, and many people enjoy amplified music because it sometimes seems possible to *feel,* as well as *hear,* it. Some of the problems of loudness are that less good musicians can shelter behind a barrage of sound, and also that some groups seem tempted to play at the same loud level all the time. This can become very monotonous, since loudness is really only effective as a contrast to softer sounds.

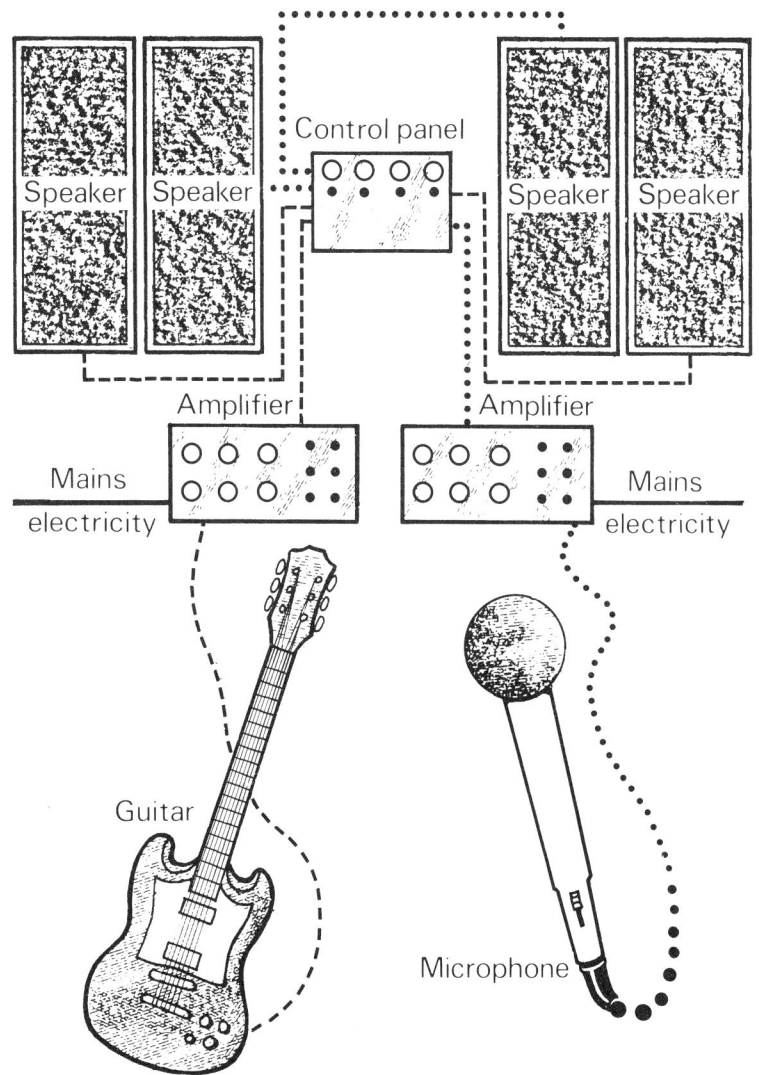

Plugging in a band: a little of what's involved

System of amplification

The system of amplification is basically simple—although with several instruments on stage (each with its connecting leads, amplifier and at least one speaker), things can go wrong. Each instrument has its **pick-up** or **microphone**, which converts the sound waves into electricity. This then passes along wires to an **amplifier**, which increases the volume (this can be adjusted); then it passes along more wires to the **speaker,** which converts it back into sound. (Actually the speaker is itself a set of speakers, some of which are for high, and some for low, sounds.)

With many bands all the instruments will be passed through a **control panel.** This allows someone who is not playing to control their volume. The control panel is particularly useful when, for example, one of the players has a part which needs to stand out from whatever else is going on. The volume can simply be turned up when needed. It is also easier to use the control panel to adjust the **balance** between the instruments for the best possible effect. For example, one hall, due to bad design, may cause bass instruments to 'boom' at the expense of higher pitched instruments. Another hall may do the opposite. In both cases careful setting of the control panel can help to improve the balance. Remember, too, that the players themselves are often not able to judge the effect their instrument is having at a distance in a strange hall.

Questions

1. What are the advantages and the disadvantages of loudness?
2. What is a control panel for?

The instruments of pop

Electric instruments

Many bands use a mixture of electric and acoustic instruments. Electric instruments are specially designed to play through an amplifier and speakers. They each have a built-in pick-up (or microphone) sensitive enough to pass on the slight sound which the instrument actually makes to the amplifier and speakers. Commonly used electric instruments include **electric guitar: lead** (six strings, tuned to **e, a, d, g, b, e**) and **bass** (four strings, tuned to low **e, a, d, g**). The range of **electric piano** and **organ** keyboards is usually less than those of acoustic instruments, although the variety of sound colours is greater. The organ shown here is the portable kind favoured by pop groups. Larger ones may have two keyboards and pedals for lower notes. The **synthesizer** is a recent electronic instrument which can be used to create any sort of sound you might want. It can sound like a violin or clarinet, for example, or produce those sound colour effects heard in the music of Pink Floyd.

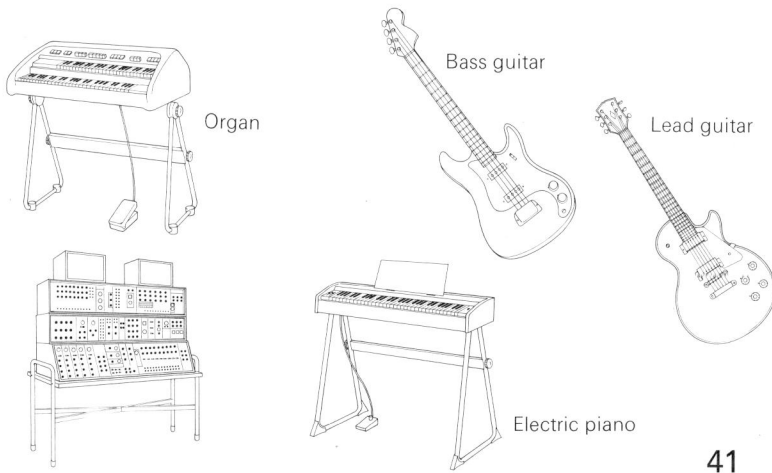

Organ

Bass guitar

Lead guitar

Electric piano

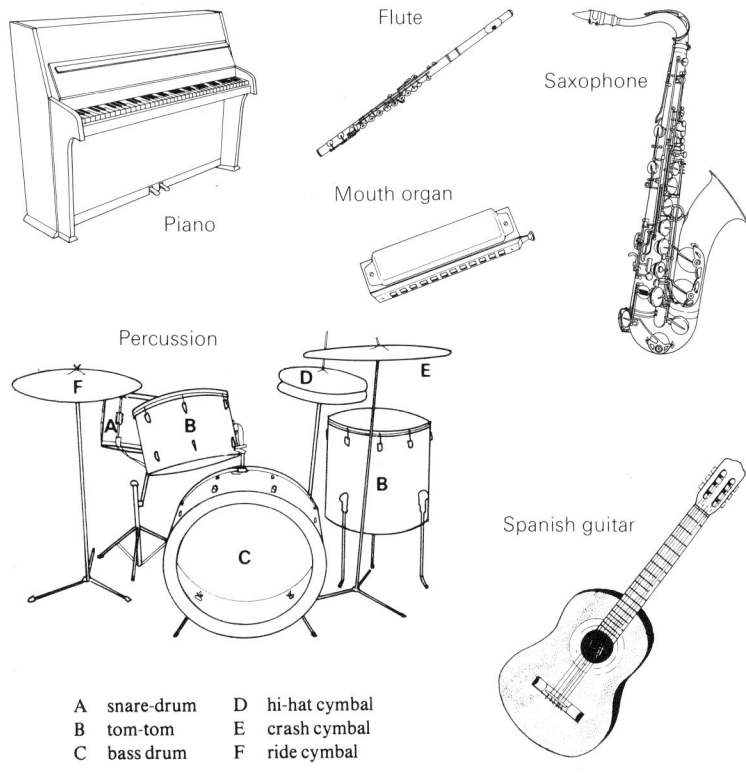

A snare-drum   D hi-hat cymbal
B tom-tom   E crash cymbal
C bass drum   F ride cymbal

Acoustic instruments

Acoustic instruments are complete in themselves and need electrical equipment only in order to be made loud enough. You can imagine how problems of balance between electric and acoustic instruments easily arise. The use of a central control panel through which all electrical circuits pass helps solve such problems.

Acoustic instruments used in pop include Spanish guitar (tuned **e, a, d, g, b, e**), violin (tuned **g, d, a, e**), saxophone, flute, mouth organ, piano and percussion. Of these guitar, violin and piano work on the principle of strings stretched across a hollow box called a soundbox, or, in the case of the piano, a soundboard, which amplifies and adds to the quality of the sound. Since both violin and piano are difficult to 'mike' satisfactorily, some players will use specially designed pick-ups. These are actually fixed to the soundbox or soundboard and can give good results. Wind instruments need separate microphones.

Since an electric guitar does not have a soundbox, like the Spanish guitar, then it is not surprising that the tone of the two instruments is very different. The same point applies to piano and organ. Musicians choose acoustic or electric instruments on the basis of which sort of instrument will sound best in a particular piece, or section, of music. And just as there are several ways of playing acoustic instruments to give different types of sound so electric instruments are provided with controls which alter the sounds, add echo effects and sustain notes.

Questions

1 What is the main difference between electric and acoustic instruments?
2 Name some acoustic instruments used in pop music.

Project

Listen to the Electric Light Orchestra's *Wild West hero* and see if you can hear the sounds of the following instruments: **bass guitar, guitar, piano, cellos, drums, violins.** Is the guitar an electric or an acoustic one? Which of the other instruments are electric and which acoustic? Why do you think the song begins with the sound of a 'honky-tonk' piano? What other sound effect can be heard very briefly at the beginning? Do you think the unaccompanied singing in the middle of the song is effective?

The recording studio

The recording studio is so important in the creation of pop music that it has become a sort of giant instrument itself. The producer of a record is a very important person, for in 'playing' this instrument he can alter the original version of a song in many different ways.

Even the smallest studio will have an eight-track magnetic tape-recorder, and the best equipped will have 16- or even 24-track machines. These recorders use 2 in. (50·8 mm) wide tape (compared with $\frac{1}{4}$ in. (6·3 mm) on domestic machines) and each track can be used to record a separate instrument or voice, not necessarily at the same time. This means, of course, that once a band has 'cut' the basic version of a song, extra performers can be brought in at a later stage to add to the effect. Glyn Johns, who has produced records for the Beatles, Rolling Stones and Who explains some of the things which can be done:

> ... you can have as many as sixteen different combinations on tape. So, when everyone's gone home you can then take what you recorded and completely change it. You run it back through the board that you recorded it through and it goes through exactly the same equipment. You can change the sound of each instrument ... You can change the perspective of each instrument by adding echo to it or taking echo away ... And, of course, you have the choice of leaving things off. For example, if there's a guitar phrase or a piano or whatever it is that doesn't work or you think you might improve it if it wasn't there, you can always take it off ...
>
> M. WALE *Voxpop* Harrap

Studio acoustics

Modern studios have to be built to take account of the many different sorts of instruments which may be used. For example, walls and floor have to be designed to absorb the strong bass guitar sounds of most pop groups; vibrations travelling through walls or floor are likely to be picked up by the microphones.

Part of the studio floor will be carpeted and instruments which are too shrill or loud placed here so that the carpet can soak up part of the sound. Another area will need to be less absorbent—probably polished wooden floorboards. A group of string players would be placed here since the polished floor reflects sound and enables the engineer to blend the instruments more easily.

To balance the sounds of the various instruments in the studio movable screens are used. These can be placed around each of the players and help direct the sounds into the microphones provided. The engineers can then relate one instrument to another as they hear them through the loudspeakers in the glass-screened **control room**, which is itself sound-proofed. Each player has a pair of earphones through which he is able to hear the sounds being produced by the other members of the group.

Mixing

Once a recording is completed it needs to be **mixed**. At this very important stage musicians and producer will finally decide about the balance between instruments, whether a certain phrase in one instrument should be made to stand out, and so on.

The mixing of a record can take days, and involves making a note of the positions of a vast number of switches, push-buttons and slider controls, each of which can affect the music. (In some studios there are even computers to help keep a check on the controls!)

Once the final mix has been decided a **master-tape** is made, from which further tapes, and later, records can be produced.

The EMI Abbey Road Studio, no. 3 control room. On the left is a 24-track tape recorder. Each track is numbered and has its own volume level indicator. (You can see these multi-track recorders at the back of the control room in the photograph below.)

To the right is a plan of the no. 3 control room.

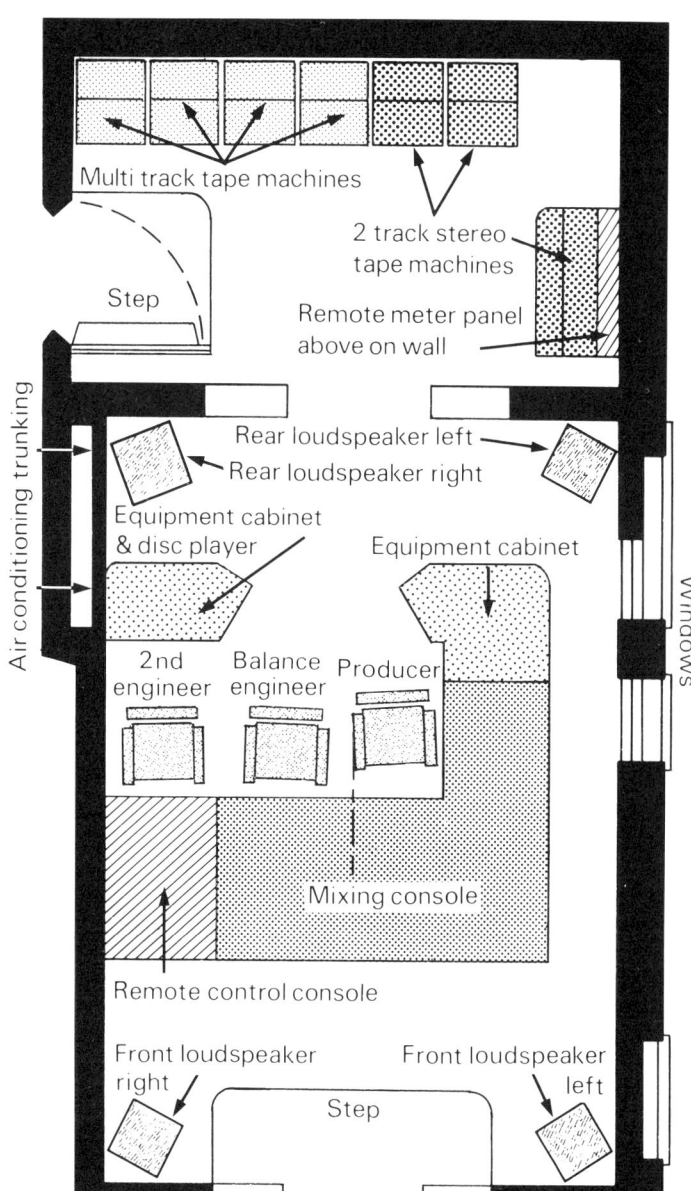

How much does it cost?

The larger studios might well employ 40 or 50 people and provide instruments for you to use ranging from harpsichords to synthesizers and guitars. There will probably also be a bar and canteen and, as you would expect, your costs will be high. If you can't afford £60, or more, per hour then you'll need to try one of the smaller studios. These supply tapes, an engineer, and an electric piano or organ and are usually capable of producing reasonable demonstration tapes (for playing to record companies who might be interested in hearing your music) at a cost of about £25 per hour.

Some pop musicians and groups—the better-off ones—use a recording studio while actually composing their material. For them the tape is rather like manuscript paper is to classical composers. Chords and melodies are recorded (written) on it, then erased (crossed out), and added to, until the basic piece of music takes shape. This explains why some groups sometimes spend months making a record and why they will sometimes build their own studios in which to do it.

Questions

1. Why have 16- or 24-track tape-recorders?
2. In a studio part of the floor is carpeted, the rest bare wood. Why is this?
3. What does 'mixing' a piece of music mean?

Project

Using any reel-to-reel tape-recorder you can lay your hands on (1) record a number of different sounds (for example coughing, clapping, whispering, laughing); play the sounds back, then (2) move the microphone and record *exactly* the same sounds again. What are the differences? (3) Having recorded the sounds try varying the speed of playback and see if people can tell what the original sounds were. These experiments will give you some idea of what an engineer can do in a properly equipped studio.

How a record is made

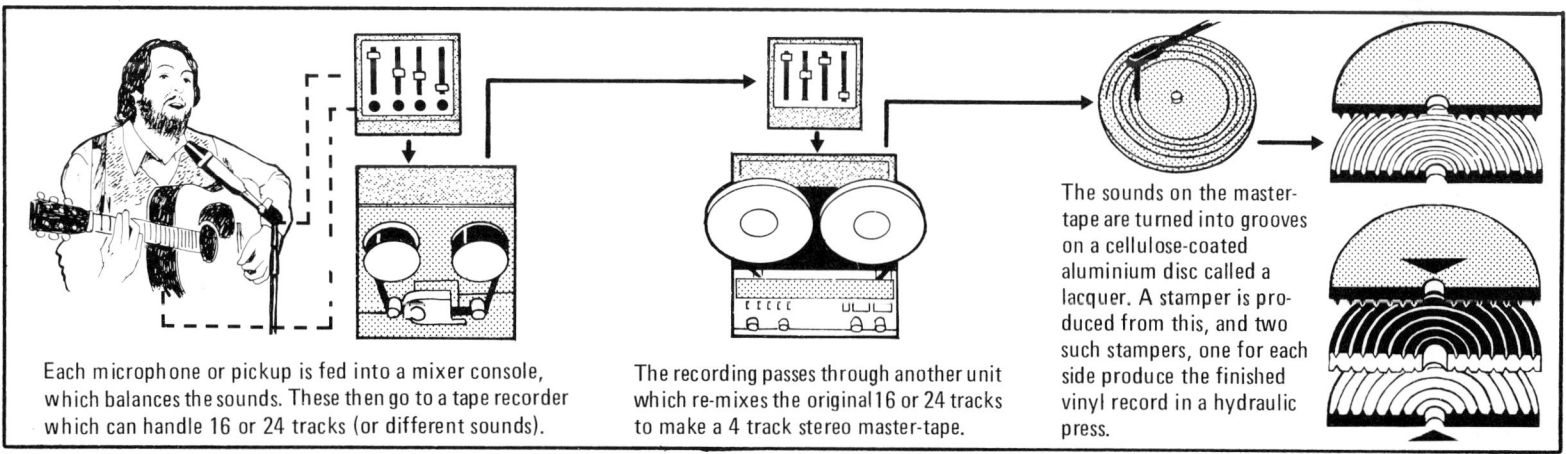

Each microphone or pickup is fed into a mixer console, which balances the sounds. These then go to a tape recorder which can handle 16 or 24 tracks (or different sounds).

The recording passes through another unit which re-mixes the original 16 or 24 tracks to make a 4 track stereo master-tape.

The sounds on the master-tape are turned into grooves on a cellulose-coated aluminium disc called a lacquer. A stamper is produced from this, and two such stampers, one for each side produce the finished vinyl record in a hydraulic press.

The Top Thirty

Each week the two leading pop music papers in Britain—the *New Musical Express* and *Melody Maker*—publish lists of the top thirty best selling single and long playing records.

Of course not all the records listed are pop music in the sense meant in this book. Frank Sinatra gets into the Top Thirty sometimes, not to mention the Muppets. But a placing in the lists can mean considerable profit for musicians and record companies, so naturally everyone involved in pop music keeps an eye on what's happening.

As you would expect, the singles list changes the most from week to week. But what is not perhaps so well known is that for some years now albums have actually outsold singles. In Britain during 1973, for example, 81 million albums were sold, and only 54 million singles.

Often a record company will release a version of a song taken from an album as a single. This then acts as a kind of 'trailer' for the album, and if it becomes a hit it will be good publicity for the group concerned. We need to remember that, although the Top Thirty singles chart is very important, it is usually the list of albums which gives the best overall idea of what's happening in pop. Some important groups, Tangerine Dream and Pink Floyd amongst them, simply do not write the sort of music which fits easily on to single records.

The hit single

What are the ingredients of a hit single? Well, Marc Bolan's first hit was *White swan*, which he described as a 'two minute, thirty second, funky, snappy, foot-tapper'. Certainly the song should not last much longer than three minutes, and it should be simple and tuneful enough for listeners to be able to remember the

Marc Bolan, whose first hit single was *White swan*

melody. The shape of the song will need to be clear and it will be repeated several times. Often there will be a short instrumental solo over some or all of the chords of the song, but it is fairly unusual for an instruments-only piece to get into the top ten. Emerson, Lake and Palmer's *Fanfare for the common man* is an exception.

	a hit single will usually
1	last no longer than 3 minutes
2	be simple
3	be tuneful
4	have a clear shape which is repeated several times
5	have a short instrumental solo

Those, then, are some of the ingredients which can help in the making of a hit single. But it's the cook who turns a recipe into something worth eating; and it's the skill of the musicians and record producer which can put those ingredients together in a way that will make their song popular enough to get into the Top Thirty. It is very important for the performers to have a definite style of their own, and if what they've produced is liked by the disc-jockeys then frequent playing on radio will help to get the record established.

How many will it sell?

For someone well-known, like the Glitter Band or Elton John, then the amount of time in the studio recording a single is not so important. The release is bound to sell well since the performer already has a following; and, although studio time is expensive, the company will still make its profit. Otherwise, the **break-even figure** is very important. This is the number of records that must be sold to get back the money which has been spent in producing the original song. It might be as low as 5000, if the band is well rehearsed and needs only, say, three or four hours to record both sides of the single. A hit single in Britain might sell between 100,000 and 150,000 copies, and a very successful one as many as 350,000, so that, once the break-even figure has been passed, there could be much profit.

Successful musicians will usually receive **royalties**, that is, a share of the selling price of each record, once profits start. Otherwise the original recording will be bought by the company from the performers for a lump-sum, and the company will have the right to do what it likes with it. The business side of pop music is very complicated, and musical values are not always the most important. Remember, too, that a pop group will need to share any profits with their manager and promoter.

Questions

1. Which sell best—albums or singles?
2. What are the ingredients of a hit single?
3. How many copies of a single need to be sold before it becomes a hit?

Projects

1. Compare the two Top Thirty singles charts taken from *New Musical Express* and *Melody Maker* of 13 September 1980. Write out a list of the important differences in placings of the same record.
2. Arrange to buy either *New Musical Express* or *Melody Maker* for two weeks running. After looking at the singles chart for the first week listen to as much of the music as you can manage and see if you can predict the second week's placings.

New Musical Express

This Week	Last Week	Title	Artist (Label)
1	(2)	Start	Jam (Polydor)
2	(1)	Ashes To Ashes	David Bowie (RCA)
3	(4)	Feels Like I'm In Love	Kelly Marie (Calibre)
4	(11)	Eighth Day	Hazel O'Connor (A&M)
5	(3)	9 to 5	Sheena Easton (EMI)
6	(5)	I Die You Die	Gary Numan (Beggars Banquet)
7	(7)	Tom Hark	Piranhas (Sire/Hansa)
7	(7)	Sunshine Of Your Smile	Mike Berry (Polydor)
9	(12)	Dreamin'	Cliff Richard (EMI)
10	(14)	Modern Girl	Sheena Easton (EMI)
11	(16)	Can't Stop The Music	Village People (Phonogram)
12	(15)	Bank Robber	Clash (CBS)
13	(10)	Winner Takes It All	Abba (Epic)
14	(—)	One Day I'll Fly Away	Randy Crawford (Warner Brothers)
15	(25)	It's Only Love/Beyond The Reef	Elvis Presley (RCA)
16	(19)	It's Still Rock And Roll To Me	Billy Joel (CBS)
17	(13)	Give Me The Night	George Benson (Warner Brothers)
18	(22)	I Want To Be Straight	Ian Dury (Stiff)
19	(9)	Oops Upside Your Head	Gap Band (Mercury)
20	(24)	Marie Marie	Shakin Stevens (Epic)
21	(8)	Upside Down	Diana Ross (Motown)
22	(18)	All Over The World	Electric Light Orchestra (Jet)
23	(29)	Paranoid	Black Sabbath (Nems)
24	(—)	A Walk In The Park	Nick Straker Band (CBS)
25	(26)	I Owe You One	Shalamar (Solar)
26	(21)	Best Friend/Stand Down Margaret	Beat (Go-Feet)
27	(17)	Oh Yeah	Roxy Music (Polydor)
28	(—)	Searching	Change (WEA)
29	(—)	United	Judas Priest (CBS)
30	(30)	You Gotta Be A Hustler	Sue Wilkinson (Cheepskate)

Melody Maker

This	Last	Title	Artist, Label
1	(2)	START	Jam, Polydor
2	(1)	ASHES TO ASHES	David Bowie, RCA
3	(7)	EIGHTH DAY	Hazel O'Connor, A&M
4	(3)	I DIE YOU DIE	Gary Numan, Beggars Banquet
5	(6)	FEELS LIKE I'M IN LOVE	Kelly Marie, Calibre
6	(5)	9 TO 5	Sheena Easton, EMI
7	(4)	TOM HARK	Piranhas, Sire Hansa
8	(11)	BANK ROBBER	Clash, CBS
9	(—)	ONE DAY I'LL FLY AWAY	Randy Crawford, Warner Bros
10	(9)	DREAMIN'	Cliff Richard, EMI
11	(10)	SUNSHINE OF YOUR SMILE	Mike Berry, Polydor
12	(15)	CAN'T STOP THE MUSIC	Village People, Mercury
13	(18)	MODERN GIRL	Sheena Easton, EMI
14	(23)	IT'S ONLY LOVE	Elvis Presley, RCA
15	(—)	GENERALS AND MAJORS	XTC, Virgin
16	(8)	THE WINNER TAKES IT ALL	Abba, Epic
17	(12)	OOPS UPSIDE YOUR HEAD	Gap Band, Mercury
18	(17)	IT'S STILL ROCK 'N' ROLL TO ME	Billy Joel, CBS
19	(20)	I WANT TO BE STRAIGHT	Ian Dury, Stiff
20	(14)	GIVE ME THE NIGHT	George Benson, Warner Bros
21	(—)	PARANOID	Black Sabbath, Nems
22	(—)	ANOTHER ONE BITES THE DUST	Queen, EMI
23	(22)	BEST FRIEND	Beat, Go Feet
24	(26)	A WALK IN THE PARK	Nick Straker Band, CBS
25	(13)	UPSIDE DOWN	Diana Ross, Motown
26	(—)	I OWE YOU ONE	Shalamar, Solar
27	(17)	ALL OVER THE WORLD	Electric Light Orchestra, Jet
28	(—)	ARE EVERYTHING	Buzzcocks, United Artists
29	(19)	MARIE MARIE	Shakin' Stevens, Epic
30	(28)	CIRCUS GAMES	Skids, Virgin

Some important names and events

Some important names and events from the history of pop music

1954-59

1954 Beginning of rock 'n' roll: Bill Haley, Elvis Presley, Little Richard
1956 Skiffle craze begins in Britain: Lonnie Donegan. Paul McCartney and John Lennon begin playing together
1957 Tommy Steele becomes popular in Britain
1959 George Harrison, Paul McCartney and John Lennon form the Silver Beatles

1960-64

1961 The Rolling Stones are formed
1962 The Beatles are formed. Bob Dylan's first album, *Bob Dylan*, released
1963 The Beatles are voted 'the world's top group' by readers of the *New Musical Express*
1964 Bob Dylan tours Britain and meets the Beatles

1965-69

1965 Folk-rock begins with Bob Dylan's concert at Newport in America and the Byrd's recording of *Mr Tambourine Man*
1966 The West Coast sound becomes popular: the Beach Boys, the Grateful Dead, Frank Zappa and the Mothers of Invention
1967 The Monterey Festival takes place
The year of the 'super albums' by the Beatles, Rolling Stones and Beach Boys
1968 Pink Floyd's album *Saucerful of secrets* is released.
Cream's last concert takes place.
Led Zeppelin is formed
1969 The year of Woodstock

1970-74

1970 The Beatles break up as a group.
Slade first play in London
1971 Carole King's album *Tapestry* is released
1972 Elton John's *Rocket man* becomes popular
1974 Mud's album *Mud rock* is released

1975-84

1975 Led Zeppelin are voted 'the world's top group' by readers of the *New Musical Express*
1976 Abba's *Money, money, money* enters the charts
1977 Punk rock begins in Britain: the Sex Pistols.
1978 Bob Dylan appears at the Blackbushe Airport concert in Britain. Also taking part: Merger and Eric Clapton (lead guitarist of Cream – see 1968)
1979 The Police's album *Reggatta de blanc* is released
1980 Kate Bush is voted 'top female singer' by readers of *Melody Maker*
1981 Reggae star Bob Marley dies
1982 Simon and Garfunkel play in London
1983 Sales of Michael Jackson's *Thriller* album total 1.6m
1984 Stevie Wonder's London concerts are acclaimed